Characters

LORD JUSTICE STEYN

MR BEGG

WAHAB AL-RAWI

JAMAL AL-HARITH

GARETH PEIRCE

MARK JENNINGS

BISHER AL-RAWI

MOAZZAM BEGG

DONALD RUMSFELD

TOM CLARK

CLIVE STAFFORD SMITH

RUHEL AHMED

JACK STRAW

GREG POWELL

MR AHMED

MAJOR DAN MORI

Guantanamo was commissioned, from an idea by Nicolas Kent, by the Tricycle Theatre in January 2004. The five British detainees were released in late February. The interviews for the play were conducted at the end of March and beginning of April 2004. Numerous attempts were made to get the viewpoint of members of the government (both in the Lords and the Commons) for this play, but no one was prepared to be interviewed.

3

The first performance of *Guantanamo: 'Honor Bound to Defend Freedom'* took place at the Tricycle Theatre, London, on 20 May 2004, with the following cast:

LORD JUSTICE STEYN William Hoyland

MR BEGG Badi Uzzaman

WAHAB AL-RAWI Aaron Neil

JAMAL AL-HARITH Patrick Robinson

GARETH PEIRCE Jan Chappell

MARK JENNINGS Alan Parnaby

BISHER AL-RAWI Daniel Cerqueira

MOAZZAM BEGG Paul Bhattacharjee

DONALD RUMSFELD William Hoyland

TOM CLARK Theo Fraser Steele

CLIVE STAFFORD SMITH David Annen

RUHEL AHMED Tariq Jordan

JACK STRAW David Annen

GREG POWELL Alan Parnaby

MR AHMED Paul Bhattacharjee

MAJOR DAN MORI Daniel Cerqueira

Directed by Nicolas Kent and Sacha Wares

Designed by Miriam Buether

Lighting by Johanna Town

Sound by John Leonard

Victoria Brittain & Gillian Slovo

GUANTANAMO
'Honor Bound to Defend Freedom'

taken from spoken evidence

With gratitude to Corin Redgrave and the families of the
British detainees and all those interviewed, without whose
help this play would not have been possible.

First published in 2004 by Oberon Books Ltd
(incorporating Absolute Classics)
521 Caledonian Road, London N7 9RH
Tel: 020 7607 3637 / Fax: 020 7607 3629
e-mail: oberon.books@btinternet.com
www.oberonbooks.com

Printed in Great Britain by Antony Rowe Ltd, Chippenham.

ACT ONE

House lights on. From the auditorium comes Lord Justice Johan Steyn, up on stage to a podium.

Written on the dot matrix: '27th F A Mann Lecture, given by Lord Justice Johan Steyn on 23 November 2003.'

LORD JUSTICE STEYN: The most powerful democracy is detaining hundreds of suspected foot soldiers of the Taliban in a legal black hole at the United States naval base at Guantanamo Bay, where they await trial on capital charges by military tribunals. This episode must be put in context. Democracies must defend themselves. Democracies are entitled to try officers and soldiers of enemy forces for war crimes. But it is a recurring theme in history that in times of war, armed conflict, or perceived national danger, even liberal democracies adopt measures infringing human rights in ways that are wholly disproportionate to the crisis. Ill-conceived, rushed legislation is passed granting excessive powers to executive governments which compromise the rights and liberties of individuals beyond the exigencies of the situation. Often the loss of liberty is permanent...

The purpose of holding the prisoners at Guantanamo Bay was and is to put them beyond the rule of law, beyond the protection of any courts, and at the mercy of the victors... At present we are not meant to know what is happening [there]*. But history will not be neutered. What takes place today in the name of the United States will assuredly, in due course, be judged at the bar of informed international opinion.

The regime applicable at Guantanamo Bay was created by a succession of presidential orders. It can be

---

* [ ] are used throughout to indicate words added to the transcripts for clarification, or to signify a cut.

summarised quite briefly. The prisoners at Guantanamo Bay, as matters stand at present, will be tried by military tribunals. The prisoners have no access to the writ of habeas corpus to determine whether their detention is even arguably justified. The military will act as interrogators, prosecutors, defence counsel, judges, and when death sentences are imposed, as executioners. It is, however, in all respects subject to decisions of the President as Commander-in-Chief even in respect of guilt and innocence in individual cases as well as appropriate sentences. It is an awesome responsibility. The President has made public in advance his personal view of the prisoners as a group: he has described them all as 'killers…'

As STEYN leaves house light dim.

The pre-dawn call to prayer: sung from the stage.

VOICES: Alaahu Akbar
Bishmillaahi-r-Rahmaani-r-Raheem
Al-hamdu Lillaahi Rabbi-i-aalameen (*Etc.*)

MR BEGG: I will start with his childhood so you have the full picture of [Moazzam].

He was born in

MR BEGG hesitates for a fraction of a second.

… '67 on 5th June and he was very well looked after by his mother and by me. When he was a little bit grown up he went to a Jewish junior school. His reports were quite good. His teachers, especially the Headmaster Mr Levy, I don't know whether he's alive or not but he was very, very good. He saw that there is good potential in my sons, so he took them after certain questions and examination. He was quite happy with Moazzam.

WAHAB AL-RAWI: (*He is smoking.*) I came into the UK in '83. [My brother Bisher], came one year later.

In the early 80's, my father was arrested – the Iraq secret service went to his office and arrested him and they took him and he disappeared for eight months. And when we found out where he was, then he was moved from one secret service to another, and he disappeared again. Eventually we found him and we used some influence at that time to just get him to go to trial. Of course he was tortured and he was abused. A year and a half he spent with the Iraqi secret service which is one of the worst in the world. Finally he went to trial. The judge found him innocent and he was released, but by then the Government has confiscated a lot of his properties and so we decided to leave Iraq for the UK.

None of us ever asked for asylum. We were very well off at the time.

MR BEGG: Moazzam did his initial schooling there and one day he said: 'Dad I want to make a society' and I smiled [because he was too young to talk about society] and said: 'what kind of society are you going to make son?' He said: 'A society to help older people, feeble people, and people with disabilities and all that.' So, I said: 'This is a very good thing, it's a noble thing. I'll not stop you doing that.' I don't know how far he went...

WAHAB AL-RAWI: I was studying GCSEs at a school in Cambridge and [Bisher] came to do the same thing. We were teenagers living on our own in one house. It's the first time we've ever gone anywhere, so it was a mess. Every day there was a fight. We'd make peace and then we'd go back and break the peace. So the next year, my mother split us apart. I went to study my A-levels in Shrewsbury and he went to Millfield College to finish his GCSEs and then do his A-levels.

[Bisher] finished A-levels, went to University. He was very physical, he was very active – this is why he loved it in Millfield – he did all the sports, wrestling, archery, climbing. Even he was a parachutist. He had 63 jumps. He had PPL – private pilot's licence. He studied on helicopters as well. Deep sea diving – he's got all the equipment for deep sea diving. He was a biker. Every sport you can imagine. If he's interested in something, then he takes it on completely. He absorbs it in his blood and veins. It's a profession. Then he leaves it and goes on to another thing.

WAITER: There's no smoking in this area.

WAHAB AL-RAWI: Oh. Okay. No problem. I'll put it out. (*Putting out his cigarette.*) I don't like to break the law.

MR BEGG: [Moazzam] was about seven [then]. Seven I think, yes he was, because it was one year before his mother died. So, he was doing this sort of thing and after one year I married again. Moazzam [was my] second born. First born had a bit of a tussle with my [new] wife (*Laughter.*) but Moazzam never had that. He was quite alright with her and he in fact supported me that we had to have somebody in the house. So, Moazzam was very co-operative. He was very, very polite, very nice, very intelligent because any question I asked he replied with proper intelligence at the age and I was surprised sometimes that he had that sort of intelligence.

After finishing the school [he] went for Law.

WAHAB AL-RAWI: [Gambia] was my idea. My idea was I build a mobile oil processing plant and because of.... obviously because of the title…because you're mobile you need to go to where the peanuts are.

MR BEGG: I'm a banker by profession [but] I opened another business [an Estate Agent] and [with] Moazzam ran [it] four or five years. Without [Moazzam] I would have not done [it]. [He] was attending the College as well at that time – going to the University part time. Then, when I finished from that business and everything he said: 'Dad, I want to get settled now. I want to get married.' I said: 'Son, I wanted you to finish these studies', as every father would think, 'and after that, you may do whatever you feel like.' He said: 'No it's all too tiring now, I can't do any more.' I said: 'Alright, take a break and next year you do what you will want to do' and he said: 'Yes, I'll do it later on.' But…er…he got married and settled down and he opened a shop, an Islamic bookshop and an Islamic clothing shop. So, that was unusual and he was running it very nicely, I think he was making a reasonable profit.

WAHAB AL-RAWI: And we decided for the experimental stages to go to a small country like Gambia and then there would be a stage two. We decided to go to Gambia because we knew somebody there. I met the first secretary for the Ministry of Agriculture and he encouraged me – I met a lot of people who encouraged me in the UK as well. I met the Gambian High Commissioner. He encouraged me – everybody encouraged me. And I thought what better to do? You go to Africa where there's poverty, you produce labour, you give these people wealth and at the same time you help yourself.

MR BEGG: [Moazzam] always used to pray in the midday because we pray, well, when I say we pray – practising Muslims I should say – pray five times a day. One early in the morning before the rise of sun, and then midday, and then we pray in the afternoon at about four or five o'clock. After that, at the time of sunset and then before going to bed. So, this five times prayer is supposed to be done by practising Muslims. I never did it (*laughter*) unfortunately. Apart from that we have got to keep fast – one month fast. So this is all good things. I don't have any objection to it, leaving that fundamentalism aside. It is not only the prayer, it is the physical exercise you do, mental exercise you do, concentration you [get].

WAHAB AL-RAWI: [My idea was] we buy the peanuts from the farmers. We process it. We produce cooking oil, which we sell back to the farmer and the by-product is animal feed which you can use to raise chicken or beef or whatever. So, everything is produced on the ground and everything is sold on the ground. And it is very, very profitable.

And my brother's position was that he was going to come over with us for a couple of weeks to help us just set the factory, build the factory – and then he'd come back. His ticket was for one month. When I asked him what he was going to do with the extra two weeks, he said, well, I'm going to go for a walkabout, see Africa.

MR BEGG: [Moazzam prayed] at least three or four times a day [and] in midday he used to put the shutter down of the shop. Not just him, there were two or three persons more used to come to the prayers. So, Moazzam prays here, in this house; in his house; in his shop; whenever he had time for prayers.

He used to call me: 'Come on down dad, this is the time of our prayer'. I'd say: 'I'm coming in a minute, I want to take a shower' (*laughter*) because you can't pray until you are absolutely clean – top to bottom and you wash your hands, you wash your mouth, you wash your face and then you wash your feet – each time – and then it's time for prayers. So, Moazzam was used to remaining very clean all the time otherwise he can't do the prayers.

[But] when he was putting the shutter down and putting the light little, people got suspicious. What this man is doing? Why the half shutter and so forth – what is he doing? So, somebody, possibly of different faith took it that something funny was going on, and informed and the shop was raided.

WAHAB AL-RAWI: I went in advance of the party to reconnaissance, to set up the company, to lease the warehouse, to lease the house for us to stay in the city, to do the banking, to get the equipment out of the port.

When I left London at the airport I was called into a room with two British officers and they interrogated me for about twenty-five minutes. They asked me: why was I going to Gambia? What did I have business in Gambia? Did I know these people – they named a few people – Abu Qatada. Did I know any Algerians? Which mosque did I frequent? All of these questions and then they were satisfied and they let me go.

MR BEGG: [The police] said that [Moazzam] must be having some connections with Taliban or somebody. He said: 'I don't, I don't know what you are talking about'. They raided his house. They couldn't get anything, nothing at all, but they were after his computer. They said there must be something in the computer, a code in computer and you have got to tell the code. [Moazzam] said: 'There is no code in computer – whatever is there is there and you can check it. You are [the] experts have it checked.' He was very unhappy. He said: ' What for are they accusing me? I know what the law is, I work according to the law, I haven't done anything wrong at all.'

[So] they took him to the court, I mean to the police station, questioned him and immediately released, and afterwards they apologised. They said we are sorry that we bothered you but we were informed or misinformed or whatever. I don't know what reason was that, but he came out very clear and there was nothing wrong and he was running his business as usual.

JAMAL AL-HARITH: I went to Pakistan on tableeg. That's sort of like when you want to find out about the religion like but you also visit villages and all that. But I didn't actually get there. It was October 2001 and I was told by the money changers, they said obviously that Americans and British wouldn't be welcome there because they were the ones who were going to be attacking, they said. Like it's 60% Pashtoun in Pakistan so they are like the people of Afghanistan. This is what I was told.

MR BEGG: I told you in the beginning [Moazzam] was very much interested to help people all the time. He somehow, had it in his mind that the Afghan people are the people in the world who are most deprived. He talked to me about it. He said: 'I want to go and start some educational institutions there'. I said: 'Who's going to back you? Do you know how the money is going to come? Is it a big project?' He said: 'No, I'll work with a small project. My wife, because they don't like mixing of woman with man or girls mixing with boys, so I'll take my wife and my wife will be teaching the girls' side of the school and I'll be teaching the boys' side.' I said: 'Well, it's a good idea if you can do that.' Then suddenly I received a letter – I was suffering from angina – I received a letter from the hospital that we have made arrangements for you to go to hospital.

JAMAL AL-HARITH: I decided to [travel] to Turkey, through Iran to Turkey. [A guy got a truck full of people] and the truck went off and then in the journey it was stopped. I was in Pakistan and then they stole the truck and I was just handed over. Gun-toting Afghanis. They didn't steal the truck to get me, they stole the truck because they wanted the truck themselves.

When the truck was being pulled over, you don't really think anything. You think, oh, they're just going to look in the truck or it's some road toll you know. That was what was crossing my mind, they were just going to check the truck or whatever. But then they just ordered everyone out, and then you know me and the driver's mate were put in their jeep or whatever to take away. Then I start to think, oh well, things aren't, you know, going as I planned – there's something wrong here, something's wrong. And obviously you're scared, your stomach's turning over and you just…

MR BEGG: Moazzam he was preparing himself to go to Afghanistan [but when] he heard that his father was going to have an operation, he came to me and he said: 'I'll drop the idea of going to Afghanistan until you are well'. I say 'No, you go. I'm in safe hands and you cannot do much here so you'd better go. I'll be alright, don't worry.' But he said 'No, this is a bad time, I need to be with you, I'll not go.'

He is a good son. He is the best son of mine. I told him 'You are wasting your time here, you are wasting your money here. They are not going to wait for you, you had better go and start the job and you can come later on, come and see me.' After about a week of intensive conversations, he somehow agreed. But he had small children. I said 'I don't particularly like that area because Afghan people are very different people as compared to us or to English people. We are more like English person: how can you live with Afghans?' He said, 'No I won't live with them, I'm teaching them but as far as living is concerned I'll be confined to my wife and children and that's it.'

He was very upset when he was going and his wife was upset too and she was crying badly that she is going. I said 'Why are you crying, what you are worried about, I'm not going to die, don't worry, I'll be alright.'

JAMAL AL-HARITH: [I was handed over to the Taliban.]

WAHAB AL-RAWI: My brother, [and my partners tried to join me in Gambia but] at Gatwick they were taken.

They were held for, I think four days altogether. Our homes were searched and the whole case went in front of a judge and the judge found there was absolutely nothing, I mean he asked the secret service why did you arrest these guys and they showed him a piece of equipment, electrical equipment and our solicitor, Gareth Peirce, she said…

GARETH PEIRCE: [One of Mr Al-Rawhi's partners Mr Al Banna had] a visit from special branch two days before he was leaving saying we know you are going. And he said do you have a problem with that? And they said no. Two days later they get to Gatwick and they're all taken off, away from embarking on the plane, their luggage searched, held on a completely false pretext for two or three days, said that there was a suspect item in the their luggage, which turned out to be a battery charger. So that we were able to go down the road from Paddington Green Police Station to Argos and get a catalogue saying here's the battery charger, while they were busy saying they were flying a forensic expert from Bali to inspect this thing.

WAHAB AL-RAWI: The judge dismissed the case.

GARETH PEIRCE: However, they then go to Gambia and are immediately arrested.

WAHAB AL-RAWI: …all of us, my brother, my two partners, myself, my driver, my contact in Gambia, we were all arrested by the Gambian secret service.

MR BEGG: [After Moazzam] went [to Afghanistan] he was ringing me up all the time from there, telling me: 'I have submitted the application to Taliban government. I'm in everything and I'm going and coming every day and there is little movement.' He felt that they are not very keen to have English or Maths or education in the country and he started getting a bit disappointed.

JAMAL AL-HARITH: [They took me to Afghanistan and] I was put in some building for three days and questioned, well not really questioned really – the main questioning was in another place. And then that's when I, you know, the kicking and all that. And then they took me out to the main prison, a political prison that they have. And then I was in isolation for two weeks but in that two weeks was when I was questioned. They asked me…where do I study, surprisingly, and all this stuff. What education have I got. Then they said I'm part of some unique special forces from England obviously, some British special forces military group that was trying to enter Afghanistan and that, er, where are the rest of the other guys, you know? And what rank do I hold in the British army? Oh and, what mosque did I go back home? Would you believe it, what mosque do I pray at back home? (*laughs*) Even the Americans asked me that.

WAHAB AL-RAWI: They took us to the secret service HQ in Banjul and they started interrogating us, it's a routine investigation. They asked us about the business. What we were coming to Gambia to do, who did we know in the Gambia? All of the stuff that were routine to the Gambians. At the end of all this two Americans came in. [They] introduced themselves as Mr Lee, and the other guy I can't remember what. Mr Lee said, I'm with the American Embassy, we're here working with the Gambians, can I ask a few questions? I said, you can't ask me anything, you have no authority over me. I want to see a solicitor. I want to see my High Commissioner. [Mr Lee] turned to the other guy and said, this guy's going to be trouble and he left the room.

JAMAL AL-HARITH: The Americans had started bombing while I was in there, and after two or three weeks I'm not sure, they released me out into the normal population, the prison population that is.

WAHAB AL-RAWI: We were separated and put in different rooms in the Gambian HQ. I was in the conference room with a mat on the floor. They told me to relax and take it easy. I was very very upset. I was shouting and screaming and being abusive. I knew that I hadn't done anything and I didn't know who had, I mean I suspected that the British authorities had ordered the arrest, but I didn't know why.

MR BEGG: One day Moazzam, he said that I have got another idea in my mind, to put in hand pumps for people living far, far away from the water source. I think that in a week's time the water was there. He called me and said 'People are very, very happy – they are dancing, they're kissing my hands, and I'm very happy'. I said 'Son, I'm happy too, that you have done that very gentle work, very high class work [but] what happened to your applications?' He said 'Well, it hasn't… I haven't got any answer to it but I'll keep on going until I haven't got funds – would you like to join me?' I said, 'When I'm well I'll come.'

WAHAB AL-RAWI: We were all moved into a house in the suburbs of Banjul. There were three or four Gambians, but I wouldn't say guarding. Don't forget this was Ramadan in Africa, so it was hot and people were fasting. It was low security. I was preparing breakfast on most occasions because the food they were bringing wasn't so tempting, so actually once I went out of the house and did some shopping on my own. Well, the guy was with me, supposedly.

[After two days] we were taken back to the Gambian secret service headquarters. [In the interrogation room] was the two Americans in front of me, and the two Gambians beside me. They went over the whole thing again and again. About the business; about who I knew.

And then after they had finished about the business, they go onto fanatical questions.

About what did I think of Mr, what is his name, not the Taliban, the Qaeda guy, what's his name…em… – Bin Laden. I said, I don't know Mr Bin Laden, you probably know him more than I do, you trained him. They said, do you know any terrorists? I said, of course I don't know any terrorists. They say that we think you have come here to do so, so and so. And I say, well this is stupid because there is no basis for that.

One idea was that [we] were in the Gambia to build a training camp. The division of labour as follows: I was the cover, going to run the business. [One of my partners] was to keep an eye on me just in case I did something wrong, so he was to be my policeman, and my brother, because of his skills, is supposed to be the trainer of the camp.

I said have you found any training equipment or military stuff? They said no. I said: my brother is supposed to be training these people but he only has a visa for one month. How can he set up a camp and train people in one month?

At the next meeting they brought another theory. We were supposed to come to the Gambia to blow up something. So I told him OK, name two targets in the Gambia that are worth blowing up and he could only name one – the American Embassy. There aren't any targets in the Gambia. Point one. Point two is: if I was coming over to blow up something, why would I come through the airport, you have two hundred miles of porous borders – no police, no nothing – I could have easily slipped through these borders. Third, where is the equipment that I was supposed to use to blow up anything? Have you found a bullet or a gun or explosives? No.

MR BEGG: Moazzam did about four water pumps in different villages, in a province called Herad. He was [putting in] the fifth one [when] the [American] bombardment started. He rushed to his house in Kabul, took his wife and children, crossed the border and came to Pakistan and during that time as there was no telephone call from him so I was very much worried – what is happening? – but he reached there and he telephoned me that we are all safe, children are all safe.

JAMAL AL-HARITH: When the Taliban, the government, fell and the new Afghan government came in to power, we were told we could leave and they were offering us money to travel to Pakistan with some guards…and I said, well, it's quicker for me to go to Kabul, thinking it would be quicker to go to Kabul because I heard the British had an embassy there. So they got hold of the Red Cross [and the Red Cross] said, okay then you stay here and we'll be in touch with the British in Kabul and then you can, you know, make arrangements to travel.

WAHAB AL-RAWI: They told us they were going to move us to a better place, I understood later they were actually using my tools and my equipment and my timber to build a jail. You heard they were boarding the windows and blocking the doors. The funny thing is they were using the food we had brought with us to feed us as well. We were hooded and handcuffed, and we were moved at two o'clock in the morning to this house one at a time. We didn't see each other.

At every single interview and every single occasion, whenever the subject comes along, I would ask to see the High Commissioner. Every single time they said the High Commissioner doesn't want to see you, sometimes they tell me, who do you think ordered your arrest? The British already knew you were in this situation.

MARK JENNINGS: I was working three days a week doing case work for Ed Davey, the local MP, and Ed happened to say to me [he had a case that] turned up to one of [his] surgeries: an Iraqi guy nabbed in the Gambia. I met the family and I got to know them as friends and it struck me that no way are they fanatical about anything. [What I learned about] Bisher was that, yes, he was reasonably devout but he's the sort of guy that can sleep for England – he used to sleep through morning prayers.

WAHAB AL-RAWI: [The Americans] had files on us. They were asking me about Abu Qatada and what Abu Qatada said about us.

MARK JENNINGS: [The connection to Bisher] is suspicious immediately because first of all, yes he's a Muslim, [and] there's Abu Qatada; also in 1998 he did a pilot's licence to fly small light helicopters, little two / four seater things, it's hardly 737s if you want to get into that, and he's a bit of a speed freak, he's got a collection of seven motorbikes, well we think there's seven – they're all in different stages of disassembly in the garage and in various places and he likes parachute jumping, he likes the adrenaline thrill. But then on the other hand he's a young man with probably slightly more money than sense so I think the only connection to any Al-Qaeda is Abu Qatada and I mean we've held Abu Qatada in Belmarsh prison for getting on for eighteen months, if not longer. We haven't been able to charge him with anything.

[With] Bisher [and Abu Qatada] certainly I think it was a friendly relationship. Bisher strikes me, from what I've heard, as being very popular with his neighbours, Muslim and non-Muslim. He's the sort of guy that's helpful. As far as I know he and Wahab, Bisher's elder brother, used to take Abu Qatada's kids swimming. I think Abu Qatada's got quite a few kids. I think the other thing they used to do was take Abu Qatada's wife to the hospital, which again is hardly the stuff of terrorism.

WAHAB AL-RAWI: One day they came into my room. Mr Lee, he came into my room and he asked me if I worked for the British secret service. I said, well I really can't answer this question, you will have to go to them and ask them politely. What kind of a question is that, I mean? So I thought about it, and I thought they must have asked him to release me.

If I tell you exactly what happened, you would never be able to come up with an answer to this problem. It's very very stupid. It's dumbfounding.

JAMAL AL-HARITH: [The Red Cross took my details] and so on, so on… Then the games began. They were in contact with the British Embassy. They said oh you know the British will be sorting something out for you. I was using the journalists' phones, they had satellite phones, so I was phoning the British Embassy all the time to speak to the guy, said yeah, yeah, we're sorting it out, you know, we're going to get either someone down, or we are going to fly you up.

[We were] constantly in touch for about over a month [then] the Special Forces came – the American Special Forces – and they questioned us to give our stories and then the Red Cross came like the day after and said like 'Oh you're going back now' said 'you're going to fly out in a plane from the American base to Kabul' and the British obviously will meet [you] there. This was arranged by them they said.

Two days before I was booked to fly out then the Americans come in and go, you know, 'You're not going anywhere. We're taking you to Kandahar' to their base.

They took me to their base obviously but put me in jail or in a concentration camp and they questioned us. Even though MI5 were there at the time in Kandahar questioning other British people that were there, they refused to see me for some reason, I have no idea what for. I spoke to some SAS guy. And then I spoke to American Intelligence – American military.

[They asked] mainly my details in England, where I lived, what jobs I had. Didn't really seem interested in anything else. Mainly just where did I work in England? At what time? My education and so on, so on. Where did I go? Where did I pray? They just seemed more interested in getting all that out than why I was here, it seemed. And the SAS guy said – he interviewed me about twice, at night, cold – he said 'I can't release you'. He didn't actually say 'You are going to be sent to Cuba', but, 'the decision is going to be with the Americans whether you get let out or not'.

WAHAB AL-RAWI: After two weeks of interrogation and threats and all of that stuff, he comes into my room, Mr Lee that is, he says, there's your passport and your ticket, you're going home, this is not a joke, we're not playing with you, you're really going home. And then he starts to relax and starts, you know, acting normally instead of the formal way.

He told me that [he had freed my one partner the day before and now, he said,] we're getting rid of you, [so] I can concentrate more on your brother.

It doesn't make sense. I'm friends with Abu Qatada, why was I let go? The whole thing doesn't make sense. If it is because we know Abu Qatada, ok, I know Abu Qatada, why release me – do you see what I mean? – and take my brother. It doesn't make sense.

MARK JENNINGS: The only difference between [the two brothers] is that Wahab al-Rawi has British citizenship and Bisher doesn't. When [they came here from Iraq] they left behind quite a large nice house plus some other assets, and they thought, well, Bisher is the youngest member of the family, if he keeps Iraqi citizenship, if there's ever a change in the regime – and I hasten to add they were very anti the war – if there was ever a beneficial change in the regime in the future, there's no problem for him as an Iraqi citizen for him to go back and say, we want our house back, thanks very much.

WAHAB AL-RAWI: Mr Lee asked me if he could keep my Iraqi passport – I had an expired Iraqi passport – and he said he wanted to keep it as a souvenir and I said no, you can't keep it as a souvenir. He said, can we give this to the guards – we had some brake pads and some expensive equipment, he said, can we give that to the guards? And I said, no you can't give that to the guards. You can give this to the guards – and we were trying to negotiate what I can keep and what I can't. And then again I was hooded, I was taken to the airport, I was taken into a lounge on my own with the Americans. We sat down talking normally and the Gambian security guard came in at that point and asked them about my property. He denied ever knowing anything about it. He said what property? I said my factory, my lorries, my equipment, my cars, my generators. He said, no we don't know anything about it, so I understood it was all gone… Altogether about a quarter of a million dollars.

[My one partner] and myself [had been held for] 27 days.

My brother and [my other partner Mr Al Banna] have been in prison ever since.

MR BEGG: [Moazzam] [and his] three children and his wife moved to Islamabad – capital of Pakistan – and they rented a flat or a house, something like that. So, he rang me up from there. I said: 'Why don't you come back now, enough is enough.' He said 'No, I've just started and I'm quite happy with it and this thing will stop in a week's time and I will go again and do that whatever I was doing and eventually I will do the school as well', but, it never happened.

Long pause.

One night two Pakistanis...two American soldiers, assisted by two Pakistani officers, burst into his house, took him as prisoner, threw him to the floor, bundled him up and put him into the boot of their car – in front of other neighbours and the little child, who is about seven now, seven or eight now, she saw that and – they took him away. I received a telephone. It was between twelve and one at night. I received a telephone call...it was whispering...I think he had his mobile with him or what ...he said – just like that

MR BEGG drops his voice and whispers.

'Dad',

Raising his voice to normal.

I said: 'Who is that?' He said:

Dropping to a whisper again.

'Moazzam'.

Normal voice.

I said: 'Why you are talking like that?' 'I have been arrested.' I said: 'By whom?' He said: 'two Pakistanis... two American soldiers and two Pakistani soldiers.' I said: 'Where are you?' He said: 'I'm in the car and they are taking me away, I don't know where. My wife and children are in Pakistan, please take care of them and don't worry,' and then either somebody saw him talking or something.

Well, I was so shocked for ten minutes I was just looking as if something had happened to my mind – it didn't work at all. I didn't know why? How? I couldn't make out anything. I couldn't make out anything.

My wife got up as well and she said 'Well, you calm down, nothing will happen'. I said 'In that [area] people kidnap people for the sake of money and they kill them and throw their bodies and take the money and so – that area is very dangerous…'

WAHAB AL-RAWI: The law in Gambia is that you can't hold somebody for more than 40 days or something like that. So, we moved immediately to get the solicitors to work on his behalf, but just before the expiry of that deadline, [Bisher] was moved with [my other partner Mr Al Banna] to Bagram airbase [Afghanistan].

MR BEGG: Moazzam said that two Americans assisted by two Pakistanis [had taken him], but who knows whether they were Americans or Pakistanis but it comes to my mind that they could be Afghans, dressed up as Americans or something. How could I think that? – that Americans will catch my son, he's from England. I couldn't think of anything like that.

WAHAB AL-RAWI: It's worse than kidnapping. It's like, if you take it from the American standpoint, we want to make sure that our people in America think that these people are terrorists. So they came not from Gambia, they came from Bagram airbase, from Afghanistan, so they must be terrorists.

We don't know exactly [how long they were held in Bagram] Because Bagram everybody knows is a no-go zone for anybody – there's no human rights, nothing.

MR BEGG: I used my resources, whatever we have in
Pakistan in army – because we come from army you see.
For generations we have been with British army so we do
not know any civil life except recently.

Some [of my relations] are quite high ranking officers. I
rang them up – I never talk to them, never took any help
off anybody in my life [but] when [the Foreign Office]
didn't give me any answer, proper answer, I rang up one
of my cousins who is Brigadier General there. I asked his
help and he straight away said: 'very sorry about it, I'll
do whatever I can.' Then I rang up General Begg who
was Chief of the Army Staff some time ago, and then I
got in touch with several officers, the high ranking
officers to search and find out if Moazzam is dead – but
nobody could find that Moazzam is dead. They said that
Moazzam is not here; he must be either as you say
kidnapped by local Patans or [he] is with Americans.

WAHAB AL-RAWI: [We got one letter from Afghanistan.]

BISHER: Dear Mother, I'm writing this letter from the
lovely mountains of Afghanistan at a US prison camp. I
am very well. The conditions are excellent and everyone
is very very nice. I hope that you, my brother, my sister
and all the family are well. Give my salaam to everyone
and I hope we meet soon. p.s. Tell

BISHER mouths a few names (to indicate censored words).

that the food is very good and I can pray as much as I
want. Your loving son, Bisher.

MR BEGG: I was like a madman for one month because
[Moazzam] was very precious to me. After one month I
receive a telephone call from Red Cross. A gentleman
called Simon rang me from a province called Kandahar.
Kandahar is next to Pakistan province – and he said 'I
am speaking from Red Cross. This is about your son. He

is in the custody of Americans and he sends you regards' – that's all. I said: 'Tell me please more', he said: 'I'm not allowed, nor I know. I can't tell you anything more.'

On one hand I was happy that [Moazzam] was alive and on the other hand I was shocked that he was in custody and I thought that possibly he is there for a week or two and then he would be released. Now, Red Cross people, Birmingham Red Cross people came down and [they] had a letter from Moazzam. We all got very excited to read the letter.

MOAZZAM: In the Name of Allah
To dad, As Salamu alaikum
I am writing this letter after around 4 wks, I am in good health and ok. I don't know what is going to happen with me, but I believe everything will eventually be ok. Please contact my wife and ask her to go back to the UK and stay with her mother. I am sorry to put you all through this, but I didn't want any of this to happen.

MR BEGG: [The letter was] from Kandahar. We wrote a reply back and gave it to the lady so that she took it away. Later on we came to know, after about two or three weeks, that he was transferred to – from Kandahar to – there's another American base which is known as Bagram, it is near Kabul. So, he was transferred there, so we think, alright, shortly they are going to sort it out or something and in the meantime we went to the Foreign Office and they say 'Well, unfortunately we don't have any access to American military bases, they won't allow anybody, so, go to the Red Cross', and that's it.

JAMAL AL-HARITH: I actually thought I was going to be released, because they said before we left [Kandahar], they said 'you have to complete the process'. The guy he said 'the process is that you are going to be [in Cuba] for one or two months and then you'll be sent home, but anyone who comes to our prison in Kandahar [has] to go to Cuba', he said. So I said 'OK then', well I didn't say 'OK', but 'if I have to go, then I have to go' and then they sent me.

End of Act One.

ACT TWO

TOM CLARK: [My sister] was very independent, capable, flexible – an enormously liberal-minded person who… she was a very…you can't talk about someone's life without saying something insipid… I don't know charming, attractive, sensible, intelligent person, enjoying her life in New York. We live[d] together for a while, for a couple of years, in New York actually, because I was studying there and my sister had a successful job and she offered to support me in my time of need. So I lived with her…first it was a kind of convenience thing and we hadn't really spent any time together since we were kids, but it worked out really really well. It was interesting, we never used to fight or argue, until we got home of course, you know what siblings are like when you put them in a domestic environment, things just go tits up. But you know it was wonderful. It was the happiest couple of years of my life, and in a way, you know I look back and know that I was very lucky to have had that – it would have been a much greater shame if I hadn't had the chance to spend so much time with her.

I don't call it 9/11, I've got an issue with that. It's not what I said before, so why should I say it now. I've always had this thing with American dates.

She's someone who worked in Public Relations, I mean it wasn't anything to do with her life, she was always politically minded, she studied Politics at college and that's what she was always going to be interested in. She got into Public Relations through working for the European Commission, I think that's how she got into it. But…it was, I don't know, I remember thinking that [injustice in the Middle East] was something we spent so much time thinking about and [she] actually genuinely cared about. And that was one of the great…the things that made me the most sad. I mean obviously her loss was the most sad thing, but all of the things peripheral to it, of all the injustices and wrongs, the fact that she actually did care about the things that led some people to think that was a smart thing to do some sort of clever stunt…that really upset me.

Call to prayer – 2nd. Noon: over loudspeaker.

MOAZZAM: [Bagram airbase]
In the Name of Allah
Dear Dad, Mum, Twins and Motard,
As-Salamu alaikum
I was very happy to receive your letter today, and I hope that you are all fine and well. Thank you for staying in touch with Sally and the children. Two letters have arrived from her and they should allow me to read them today or tomorrow. I have been extremely worried about them, and don't know even if they were left with any money. Please, help them in whatever way you can and I will repay you as soon as I can. Don't let my children want for anything due to any financial problems. I am doing well here and treatment has been good. Food, water, clothes and Quran are all provided. I am now about to complete my 7th reading of the Quran, and have memorised many chapters, praise be to Allah. The days go by slowly, but my ability to speak English has been a tremendous help. I cannot tell you much about what is going to happen, but I remain patiently hopeful and pray that soon I will see you all again. This is the hardest test I have had to face in my life and I hope I have not caused you too much distress, but I will pass this test by the will of Allah and your prayers. I love and miss you all very much. I thank you for all that I never did thank you for (both you and mum).
Your loving son, Moazzam.

DONALD RUMSFELD in press conference.

NEWSPAPERMAN 1: Mr Secretary…

NEWSPAPER MAN 2: Mr Secretary…

RUMSFELD: We were able to capture and detain a large
number of people who had been through training camps
and had learned a whole host of skills as to how they
could kill innocent people – not how they could kill
other soldiers. We've got a good slug of those folks off
the street where they can't kill more people.

*BISHER AL-RAWI is putting on the orange boiler suit of
Guantanamo marking his transition from Bagram to
Guantanamo.*

BISHER: Dear Mother,
I'm writing to you from the seaside resort of
Guantanamo Bay in Cuba. After winning first prize in
the competition, I was whisked to this nice resort with all
expenses paid. I did not have to spend a penny. I and
Jamil [Al Banna] are in very good health. Everybody is
very nice. The neighbours are very well behaved. The
food is first class, plenty of sun and pebbles, no sand I'm
afraid. Give my salaam to everybody and my special
salaam to Wahab. I wish him the very best with his life,
religion and business. I hope to see you soon if you
want. Your son, Bisher.
p.s. Please renew my motorbike insurance policy.

RUHEL AHMED is wearing the boiler suit.

RUHEL: Assalamwa-alakum
Hi, how are you all. I'm fine and well. I recieve your
letters and photos. Well about my eyes u can send me
contact lenses. Get them from Sandwell hospital [Eye
Clinic] and solution for Boots. Its call [Boston advance
care]…and I need protein tablets to clean them… [Total
Care tablets for hard contact lenses]. Both solution and

tablets for hard contact lenses. Its going to cost total of £30.00. I need 2 packets of tablets and 1 packet of solution. You don't need to worrie about me. They army cool with me and everyone. Well what can I say to u all. The solders call me by the name of Tiger and Slimshady for some reason. Im know very well. All the army know me as U know everyone me back home as I used to be centre attration where ever I went. ...Hope to see you very soon inshallah, assalemalaykum, love Ruhel Ahmed.

RUMSFELD points at one of the newspaper men.

NEWSPAPERMAN 1: But have you determined [the detainees'] status individually, on an individual?

RUMSFELD: Yes, indeed, individually.

NEWSPAPERMAN 1: So you know which are al Qaeda and which are Taliban?

RUMSFELD: 'Determined' is a tough word. We have determined as much as one can determine when you're dealing with people who may or may not tell the truth.

NEWSPAPERMAN 1: Right.

RUMSFELD: So yes, we've done the best we can. They are not POWs, they will not be determined to be POWs. Don't forget we're treating these people as if the Geneva Convention applied.

GARETH PEIRCE: There are a number of concepts which are deliberately confused by the American administration. It seized people for purposes that are clearly the obtaining of information and having seized those people, it transferred them to a place which it believed would be beyond the reach of courts in America. It claimed that it had seized people on the battlefield, there were frequent references to capture on the battlefield, and then, having presented it to the world in this way, found itself stuck with the immediate response, well if these are prisoners of war, they are entitled to give name, rank and number and no more, and they deserve to be treated as the Geneva Convention dictates and not to be made the subject of interrogation. So having at first flush grabbed the nearest label, finding that it meant that there were international treaty obligations to provide prisoners of war with rights, the regime very quickly had to redefine what it had, and therefore it said these were unlawful combatants who were not wearing uniform and were not conforming to the norms of warfare.

RUMSFELD: We said from the beginning that these are unlawful combatants, and we're detaining them. We call them detainees, not prisoners of war. We call them detainees. We have said that, you know, being the kind of a country we are, it's our intention to recognise that there are certain standards that are generally appropriate for treating people who were – are prisoners of war, which these people are not, and – in our view – but there – and you know to the extent that it's reasonable, we will end up using roughly that standard. And that that's what we're doing. I don't – I wouldn't want to say that I know in any instance where we would deviate from that or where we might exceed it.

MOAZZAM: [Bagram airbase] [To Sally Begg]
In the Name of Allah, Most Compassionate Most Merciful
Dearest Zaynab, As-Salamu alaikum
I am writing this message late at night, which is usually when I cannot sleep, because of thinking and worrying all the time, the heat and bright lights. I have written several messages to you and it appears that you have not received any except the first one! Please let me know exactly what messages you got (the date I wrote on the

message) and I will see what has happened. These past few weeks have been more depressing than usual especially since the birth of our son, May Allah bless and protect him and all my family. Time is dragging on so slowly and things don't change here at all, if they do it is very slowly. I still don't know what will happen with me, where I will go and when, even after all this time! There is nothing here to do to occupy time, except read the Quran which I have finished so many times. There are many rules here which does not make this wait any easier. The food has been the same for 5 ½ months, 3 times a day, first meal in the morning and last in the late afternoon, and most of the time I am hungry. I miss your cooking so much.

MOAZZAM mouths words (censored words).

The most difficult thing is my wife being away from you and the kids, and being patient.

MOAZZAM mouths words.

I miss you and love you as much. Moazzam

CLIVE STAFFORD SMITH: I run a [legal] charity called Justice in Exile in the US, which is devoted to representing the people in Guantanamo Bay. Guantanamo Bay is a massive diversion. It's got nothing to do with the real issues – none of [the people that they think are] the real bad dudes are in Guantanamo Bay, because the American Government would never put them there while there is a possibility that we'll get jurisdiction to litigate to get them out of there. So all of them are in Bagram air force base and places like that.

GARETH PEIRCE: [There are] 700 in Guantanamo, [there are] however many thousands around the world, distributed in places where Guantanamo would probably look quite humane. And there is a process of shipping people for instance to Egypt, where you know they'll be tortured. [You] torture something out of them, then get them back to Guantanamo. [It's] a grotesque international redistribution. And what are you getting out of it? Well maybe that's where the weapons of mass destruction came from. Certainly the product you'll get is bound to be complete nonsense, bound to be, once it's ricocheted off 700 people, any cocktail of invention will have happened.

RUMSFELD: Anybody who has looked at the training manuals for the al Qaeda and what those people were trained to do, and how they were trained to kill civilians – and anybody who saw what happened to the Afghani soldiers who were guarding the al Qaeda in Pakistan when a number were killed by al Qaeda using their bare hands – has to recognise that these are among the most dangerous, best trained vicious killers on the face of the earth.

NEWSPAPERMAN 3: Mr Secretary, there was a debate…

RUMSFELD: And that means that the people taking care of the detainees and managing their transfer have to be just exceedingly careful for two reasons. One, for their own protection, but also so these people don't get loose back out on the street and kill more people.

RUMSFELD points at NEWSPAPERMAN 3.

NEWSPAPERMAN 3: Mr Secretary, there was a debate yesterday in the British Parliament. I happened to notice.

RUMSFELD: Oh I read some of that. Just amazing.

NEWSPAPERMAN 3: And it – well it was interesting. And one of the comments made was that [the] handling of John Walker, a United States citizen, has been different from the handling of the others, and that this demonstrated that the United States would not treat one of its own people the way that it has treated these others. And I would ask your reaction to that?

RUMSFELD: Well, it's amazing the insight that parliamentarians can gain from 5,000 miles away. I don't notice that he was handled any differently or has been in the past or is now.

NEWSPAPERMAN 3: Well, will he be put in an eight by eight cell that has no walls but only a roof?

RUMSFELD: The…just for the sake of the listening world, Guantanamo Bay's climate is different than Afghanistan. To be in an eight-by-eight cell in beautiful sunny Guantanamo Bay, Cuba is not a – inhumane treatment. And it has a roof. They have all the things that I've described. And how each person is handled depends on where they go. And Mr Walker has been turned over to the Department of Justice. He will go where they want him. He will not go to Guantanamo Bay, Cuba.

Points to NEWSPAPERMAN 4.

NEWSPAPERMAN 4: On a related question, there are British citizens at Guantanamo Bay.

RUMSFELD: Yeah.

NEWSPAPERMAN 4: Can you clarify – did the United States tell the British government about moving these detainees from Afghanistan to Guantanamo Bay? That we were taking this step?

RUMSFELD: I don't know, my – the United Kingdom is working very closely with us. They have liaison in Tampa, Florida. They are part of the coalition. They're leading the international security assistance force. People talk at multiple levels with the UK every day of the week, every day of the – just continuously. And do I know whether someone called them up on the phone and said: Gee we're thinking of doing this, that, or the other thing? I just don't know the answer to that. You could ask them.

NEWSPAPERMAN 4: Well their claim is that they weren't told, and they seem pretty upset about it. And I'm just wondering...

RUMSFELD: 'They' – who's 'they'?

NEWSPAPERMAN 5: Several members of the British parliament are claiming that the British...

RUMSFELD: They are not the government. The 'they' is the UK government, and if I'm not mistaken, I read that Prime Minister Blair and the other representatives of the government said things quite the contrary to what you're saying.

RUMSFELD points at Newspaperman.

RUMSFELD: Yes.

NEWSPAPERMAN 5: Mr Secretary, you've said that you reserve the right to hold the detainees until the end of the war. You've also said that there won't be a signing ceremony on the Missouri in this war.

RUMSFELD: Right.

NEWSPAPERMAN 5: So when exactly is the end of the war? And are we talking about the war on terrorism or the conflict in Afghanistan?

RUMSFELD: Well, at the moment, we all know the conflict in Afghanistan is going on, so we're not past our deadline or our due date. I don't know how to describe it, and I suppose that will be something that the president would make a judgement on, as to when it was over.

MOAZZAM: [Bagram airbase]

...When I wrote about all those insects etc – that was in the Summer; now it's well into Winter. The camel spider is the only 10 legged spider in the world, and, I believe, is not an arachnid: (technically not a spider). But it grows to bigger than the human hand-size, moves like a race car and has a bite that causes flesh to decay – if untreated. In the Summer there were plenty here, running into the cells and climbing over people; one person was bitten and had to be treated. Apart from that, there is the usual melee of scorpions, beetles, mice and other creepy-crawlies. Thank God it's Winter! I have done a lot of reading in the past few months (45 books or so); just having read about the US Wars of Independence and Civil War.

MR BEGG: I received a telephone call from the Foreign Office...and the person in charge of the case she told me that [Moazzam] has been transferred to Guantanamo Bay from Bagram air base... It was a surprise yes. I was not expecting him to go there. I was expecting that he was going to be released. He's an innocent person and he didn't do anything wrong as far as we know, and so I thought that possibly he's going to be shortly released. And then I received a message that he was going to Guantanamo Bay, that he'd been transferred to Guantanamo Bay.

[Moazzam's] oldest daughter here, she understands. She understands that her father has been taken away by Americans and they...she gets at times nightmares. She says at times, 'my father is being beaten up, his head is bleeding'.

JAMAL AL-HARITH: When I first arrived [in Cuba], they put me in a block where there was some English people there from Birmingham, the guys from Birmingham or one from London, or two from London. I was only there for an hour, because when I came in, obviously the plane journey with a mask, and everything, and goggles, I nearly fell out there unconscious from the plane. [Then they] moved me to the hospital. The guy took blood pressure and x-ray and then he just gave some tablets. Didn't say anything apart from 'How do you feel now?', I said 'OK', 'No, how do you feel?' and I said 'like my muscles are just relaxed'. He had given me a muscle relaxant. And he said 'Oh your blood pressure was one of the highest I've seen here'. But the reason why was cos the chains on my foot.

You had four or five different types of chains. It depended on how your interrogation was going to go. If they came with chains that made you sort of hunch up and have to walk like that then you knew they were going to be hard on you when you get to the interrogation. Or if the chains were where you can actually stand up, easier and walk, then they want something from you, so there're going to be nice, and they might offer you tea or something like that, or a drink of water.

The Americans would change their interrogators every three month, so you had new interrogators coming in. The British, some of the guys would come back again, but mainly you'd get someone different each time with the ambassador he would come. Round about six or seven times, I was interviewed by them. But the British, they didn't come just for us. Cos they were like given free rein in the Camp. Anyone like who had took a transit in England and spent like an hour on a plane, stopped in England for an hour, were questioned by the British.

GARETH PEIRCE: I think slowly the world has become aware that Guantanamo Bay is a convenience, it's a resource pool for American intelligence, and even more disturbingly perhaps, the intelligence services of the rest of the world, who are deemed to be allies, or even those who are perhaps not deemed to be allies. There is a huge range of nationalities captured there.

JAMAL AL-HARITH: I found a lot of the guards were stupid. Just young coming in like they were in training, and I would say to them, especially when they said 'Oh, we've put your name and your picture through like Interpol, all the Intelligence Agencies of the world or whatever, First World countries, and nothing came back on you, you haven't even got a parking ticket. I said 'That's because I haven't done anything'. And I said 'You know I'll walk out from here when I leave, free, because I haven't done anything at all, but your problem is that you've got me here and you can't release me without having something on me.'

They have these names they use. In [Delta] it was 'reservation'. 'You're going for reservation.' It means interrogation, but they didn't like to use the word 'interrogation'. 'You're not really being interrogated, we're investigators.' They use all these words. In Delta it was – no sorry in X-Ray it was 'exhibition'. 'You're going for exhibition' this meant interrogation.
They use words but there's evil behind it man. There's malice.

Pause.

I got put in isolation for [the first time], because I refused to wear my wrist band. I said 'In concentration camps they were given tattoos, and now they've given us these, it's just the same really. I said 'As a matter of principle', I'd keep saying 'As a matter of principle' – I'd keep saying it, and that would easily get me into trouble. So as a matter of principle every time they gave me a wrist band, I'd rip it off. The cages [had] little bits sticking out, I'd just put the band on it until its cut then I'd rip it off and [then] I used to throw it out. And this went on for a couple of weeks, and after a certain time they just said 'We've had enough, mate', so they put me in isolation for four days.

They took me in chains out down to isolation. There was nothing in the isolation cell except bare metal – just like a freezer blowing cold air for 24 hours, so it turns it into a freezer box, a fridge. I had to go under the metal sheet because the cold air was blowing in. I tried to go to sleep but you can't because you're just shaking too much. I said, oh I can't do this to myself. I said I can't do this.

Some people admitted to stuff in Kandahar, because of the beatings and they used electricity on some of the people there as well, but in Cuba they changed their minds, they said 'Oh no, what we said wasn't right. It isn't true'. I know some people signed papers, but I don't know what they signed. I know under pressure that people have admitted to stuff, but I said 'No way, am I doing that'. I mean without being arrogant, but internally I am mentally stronger than a lot of people.

CLIVE STAFFORD SMITH: We have learnt shocking things. For example in the first few months at Guantanamo they had 32 suicide attempts and then suddenly the suicide attempts [seemed to stop]. There was effort on behalf of the powers that be down there to act as if, ah, everyone's calmed down now, they're taking their Prozac, there's no problem. But then we discover that far from suicide efforts stopping, they'd just been re-classified by the military into Manipulative Self-Injurious Behaviour. There were more than 40 of those in a six month period, since the re-classification of suicide attempts.

MR BEGG: It's very personal but I'll tell you [this]. I talk to [my son]. Because I love him. When you are in deep love with somebody you tend to talk to him – in your dreams, in your life, when you are alone.

At times I see that he is sitting here and I'm shouting, and he puts his head down, and quietly listening to him. He's a grown up man, he's a married man, he's got children, he's a responsible person and I was shouting at him – telling him off – [and he just sits there].

WAHAB AL-RAWI: The times that are awkward are when you're on your own at night, when I don't sleep, and then you start to say what can I do, is there anything I can do, and you end up on a nightmare, and I keep getting these stupid nightmares. Just ugly ones – I'm walking in a tunnel, and I turn to my left and just near the staircase my brother is there and he's getting beaten up by four guys, and he just turns to me, and he doesn't say anything, he just turns to me and gives me this look, as if 'why aren't you doing anything about it?' and I wake up sweating and angry and I just want to punch something. You tell me what can I do about it?

JAMAL AL-HARITH: I used to sometimes think 'Gosh, I'm from Manchester, what am I doing here?' I'd look at the cage, and think 'Is Beadle going to come round or something.'

I had a dream a year in that I was going to stay there for two years. And that's one of the big things in there – dreams. People had dreams and they would tell it to everyone, and raise everyone's spirits. So dreams was a big thing, and you had interpreters of dreams as well there.

In Kandahar, I [dreamed] myself back home, watching the news, with some guys about Cuba. So I said 'That's the sign for me that I'm going back home'. And I would take it as a sign that's my personal sign to me that I'm going back home. But some people would say 'No, you can't take it, it's just a dream' and I'd say 'No, no'. You have to hang on to something, because that was my hope. I freely admit that when I did see that dream, I said to myself 'I know I'm going back home'. And I just had to keep on believing. No-one swayed me on that.

JAMAL AL-HARITH: I did more worship [in Guantanamo] because you're in that situation, you just do, you don't have a choice but to have patience, because you can't do anything. But I did do a lot more worship – at night praying and so on. I think if I didn't then I would have been mentally more affected. It was a release for me. It was something to hang on to.

Call to prayer – 3rd. 4pm: over loudspeaker.

RUHEL AHMED: ...the US army has made a new prison. We got tranfered here on 27/04/2002 and its better in some ways. We have a toilet and a bed. We hardly see the sun or moon anymore cause we are in side buildings in the old prison it used to be open air u could see different animal and stuff like that.

All of u pray all time not for me, for urselfs cause on day of judgement u all have to answer for ur own actions and deed. No one will want to know anyone on that day. Are you excesizing Shian, Junel and Juber. Keeping healthy if not start, stay in shape. Me myself excercis all day long about 4 hours a day. Got a nice pack of six pack now & looking good as always. Mom and Dad How are U. I hope u all forgive for the pain I brought too u both in these last few years. I know I haven't been a good son. Hope u can forgive me. Luv u all and miss u. inhsallah. See U soon. Assalamwaalaykum. Luv Ruhel.

CLIVE STAFFORD SMITH: [I've done death penalty work] for the last 20 years. It's all about hatred. About how you get a huge group of people to hate a small group of people and in that way you get them to quit blaming their problems on the Government. You hate black people because that avoids you blaming the Government for your own problems, and [you] hate people on death row and blame them all for the problems in the world.

[But] OK, [so] we hate people on death row. If they hate us back, it doesn't have any impact, because they have no power. Yet when we translate this onto [Guantanamo, and] the international stage, and we hate Muslims, and let's be honest that's what's going on here, despite the pathetic attempts to pretend that's not true. There are one billion Muslims around the world, and when we [hate them] we create a world which is a very very dangerous and unpleasant place. Translated onto the international scene, it's terrifying.

WAHAB AL-RAWI: I am angered by my Government and I don't see what difference is between Saddam Hussein and Bush and Blair. Saddam Hussein did exactly the same thing to my country and that is why we came there and we came here and we end up with the same misery – ten times over – because this is supposed to be a land of freedom and laws.
I even thought about putting [on] a suicide belt, but that doesn't help [Bisher]. But that doesn't help him. That doesn't help anybody.

TOM CLARK: I remember thinking more about the Guantanamo Bay thing – when you mentioned you were doing this, I sort of thought, well, what do I think, what is my attitude because it changes and it swings over time. But, you know, [my sister] would have been incensed.

…But then, she, you know, was incinerated publicly, live on television, for an hour and forty minutes…

Let's say for the sake of argument that among those detained at Guantanamo Bay are some of the people who led to her death – who murdered her essentially – that's

43

a little difficult for me to, you know, it's difficult for me to say it was a bad thing that they were there.

Suicide bombing is a completely bizarre thing. It is...if there was such a thing as evil, I've lost the belief that there is...but if there was, that would be the most evil thing. So yeh, lock 'em up, throw away the key.

JAMAL AL-HARITH: [I stopped talking to the guards], because I couldn't justify myself laughing and joking with them, [after] they're beating upon this guy, I turned away from them. I wouldn't communicate with them. Sometimes I wouldn't even ask for salt. And the guys through the holes in the cells, used to pass me salt and so on, because they knew that I had a principle that I was not going to back down on.

[There's one detainee] an Arab. They hate him, the guards, the Americans, hate him. Because he organised. If someone was in trouble, say not giving medicine to someone, cos if you were ill they wouldn't give you medicine until you drop out or there's blood, because then it's not counted as serious. So if you're in pain, it doesn't matter, be in pain. He would, if it was in his block, say: 'Right, no-one's taking food', or: 'We're not going off to showers, no-one's going to go in interrogation', and everyone would just stand firm and say 'We're not going until this guy gets seen to by a doctor', and we had to do that quite a few times as well.

That same guy [who] organised people said like every block's got to have an Emir that people if people have a question you ask. And then if something happens everyone gets together, because only when you get together can you stay strong and sane. So they try to implement it but anyone who was elected Emir would get put in isolation. So they were trying, and then the thing is [that guy], he read the Geneva Convention in

Arabic, and it said that you are allowed to do this, I think it was Red Cross someone said you are allowed a leader. But the Americans said 'There's no law here, it does not apply'. So when we tried to organise Emirs, they kept putting them [in isolation] so people were afraid to become Emir now. So [we] tried to use codes, and one of the codes was like 'Have you got a cook in your block?' Yeah, Yeah'. 'No, we haven't got a cook', 'Well you need to get one.'

RUHEL AHMED: …It's getting hot again here as summer is around the corner. Bros getting married which I cant belive and Im stuck in Fucking Cuba mind my French couse it bad… Everytime I write a letter I can't think what to write. Suppose don't do anything here except the same thing day in day out. I myself don't know how long its going to be until come home but Inshallah soon.

TOM CLARK: [So] Part of me is like, yeh, throw away the key, let 'em rot. Who gives a shit really?
Part of me wants to say it's completely fine. [But] another part of me [wants to understand why] have they been detained for so long. I mean what the hell have they been doing up there? The American Government put a ridiculous amount of resources into this, they've got so much money to spend on the war against terror surely, they could have them processed quicker? Surely, they could figure out which ones? At least if they decided they needed detaining in some way, to do it in the eyes of, either their own people or an international court or something, at least to illustrate what they're doing to these people, why they're detaining them longer because, although their initial reaction I think I'm comfortable with, given the extremes, I can't understand why detain them for longer.

If I had to sum up, it would be: I'm furious at the length of detention of these people, furious because those who are innocent have lost three years of their life, much as I lost, as I've been living in a sort of private hell since my sister was murdered, and although at least I've been able to recover and get over it and deal with, and still sort of have my life, they've had theirs taken away. And that's …and they'll never get it back and I'd buy them a drink if I met them, you know, if in truth they had done nothing wrong, I can't imagine a worse thing for any person, they deserve all of our sympathies and all of our efforts to sort of make sure they do actually get the justice that they deserve.

End of Act Two.

ACT THREE

Call to prayer (sunset – the prayer itself, or first two stanzas, out loud: last one silent): over loudspeaker (or from stage).

On dot matrix: 'The Minister of State for Foreign Affairs, the Right Honourable: Jack Straw. MP. February 2004.'

JACK STRAW: Good afternoon. I am going to make a statement concerning the nine British citizens detained at Guantanamo Bay.

In July 2003, two of the British detainees were designated by the United States authorities as eligible to stand trial by the United States Military Commissions.

The British Government has made it clear that it had some concerns about the Military Commission process. Consequently, the Prime Minister asked the British Attorney-General to discuss with the United States authorities how the detainees, if prosecuted, could be assured of fair trials which met international standards. Our discussions are continuing.

In the meantime, we have agreed with the United States authorities that five of the British detainees will return to the United Kingdom They are:

Ruhel Ahmed
Tarek Dergoul
Jamal Al Harith
Asif Iqbal
Shafiq Rasul

GREG POWELL: So finally Jack Straw tells us that my client Ruhel Ahmed is going to be released, but there is no date given. So what you have is journalists ringing me up saying it's going to be whenever. Tuesday and it's going to be at Northolt Airport, and they should arrive at 8 o'clock on a plane. Well it's news to me you know, because no-one tells the lawyers. It's all been leaked out to [the] Press, who then ring the lawyers and tell you, and then you ring the family and tell them, then you ring the Liaison Police Officer and tell him and he says 'Well, I don't know about that', then he has to then ring somebody else and find out about it. At the airport the backpacker Jamal, who has been jailed by the Taliban and then handed over to the Americans, is released.

JAMAL AL-HARITH: If I am the worst of the worst, and obviously the scum of the earth, and people should fear me, of course, why then have they been released? After two years in there, I mean they still didn't give me a reason for being in there.

GREG POWELL: The other four, which include the Tipton three, are taken off to Paddington Green to be interviewed by the anti-terrorist squad. When we arrive at the freezing cold Paddington Green Police Station foyer, [there are] thousands of policemen outside, and they've got Press and they've got barriers up, and created a one-way system round the police station, high security and all that.

It was maybe half ten by the time we had finished the booking in procedure. And all the Police are going to do, they tell us, is take fingerprints and DNA and that's going to be it for the night. [But first] we have this farce over fingerprinting. We go into a little fingerprint room [with] quite a large officer, who is fat and a bit tired, and obviously hasn't taken fingerprints for a long, long time. There is no live-scan computers: they are going to do it on a Victorian ink block. So he gets out the ink block and inks it all up, but the block doesn't quite fit on the little spindle. It's not quite stable and it rocks. And he's got lots of bits of paper, and he's going to put fingerprints on them. He is putting the right hand ones on [when he sees] he's [using] the left hand piece of paper. He start(s) again with the left hand piece of paper and he [sees] that he has done the right hand.

The [trick is to] take the finger and roll it in a certain way,

GREG POWELL now using his index finger to demonstrate.

make a certain movement with it, [but] because he had not done it for a long time, he's not very good. He [can't get] clear images. So he gets another officer to help, then [one more] officer turns up to help him [with] a Finger Print Case [and a] different roller. [And all] this takes over two hours to do. The officer is getting hot, he's beginning to sweat and knowing he's having to do it again, and he feels really uncomfortable because it is all humiliation for him: there's this high-tech, top of the tree, top class, anti-terrorist squad officer taking over two hours to fingerprint somebody. Not to mention the bits of paper, you can't imagine how many bits of paper there are in this room at this point. [My client] is trying his best to help. At one point [they decide] that the thing is too low and they put it up on another piece of board, and [my client] is twisting his fingers, and doing his stuff, and the officer is getting ink on his shirt, and I say to them at one point: 'I'm sure I've seen something like this on Blue Peter'.

It was the biggest farce really, at the end of it, can you imagine, two and a half years in Guantanamo Bay, you arrive back in the country, you go to Paddington Green High Security Police Station and you end up you know at 1a.m. with this pile of fingerprint paper and this officer up to his knees in Victorian ink. The next day all four which include my client Ruhel are released, so the three boys from Tipton can finally go home.

GARETH PEIRCE: One of them, the tallest of them, has problems with his joints, real problems, because the space in which they had to exercise. And one of the young men had problems with his eyes, a particular dislocation of his eyes, which require contact lenses, they require them to stop something horrible happen[ing] to the eyes, he hasn't had them for two years. Ultimately the eye breaks if it isn't held in.

MR AHMED: [When I first go to meet my son, Ruhel after he came back from Guantanamo I thinking of him like] a small boy. [Before he went he had], no hair, no beard. Now he have very long beard up to there…

Gestures down almost to his waist.

I'd like to cry but I can't cry. I do not cry. He look like people who walk around the streets. I don't cry.

My heart filling, I see my boy like it was two years, I want to hold him, I want to cry myself, but I can't do it. [When somebody] hitting you, you can cry, somebody beating you, you cry – but without reason you can't cry, but when I see him in this condition I'm surprised… I did. I did want to see him. But how I'm supposed to think when he look like this?

[I] want to cry but I don't know how. He said to me: now give me telephone. I say to him, I give you mobile and he [press the numbers like this].

MR AHMED holds up a make-believe mobile to show how his son held his face really close to the phone – illustrating how bad RUHEL's eyes are.

and then my cry comes out. [And] I don't want it coming out… This make me so upset because he is my son, he is a young boy and I am old man… [and] …he could not see anything. So I am crying myself. And he said don't cry, this time is gone.

MR AHMED drops his voice.

Don't cry, it will be alright.

On the next night…we go with his mother – we were crying everybody… He say, don't worry Daddy I'm OK, don't cry… He's got less feeling, less feeling than before. He always talk. He always talk.

Two nights he stay here. The whole night he walks. He walk himself…around the house…from there. To there.

Gesturing.

I left him here.

Pats the sofa.

If he's coming home, I have no room, over two years now we are all set up so I have no room for him. So I said to him, you go to my bed. I said: Me and my wife sit down here and you go of my bed. He say; 'no, mine's too [big]. I need small room. Small places, I don't sleep all night.' He say: 'I'll close my eyes and sit down, I'll be OK.' He could not sleep apparently. So, he walk round all night… I've been to bed, come back five o'clock… He walk round here.

Indicating how RUHEL walked.

Walk round here…I say: 'what you doing?'… So I said go on, go to my bed, so he go to bed. Nine o'clock he come back…

GARETH PEIRCE: The [boys] are three young British lads who are like all our children – they're people who are very familiar, very easy to feel immediately comfortable with. And yet the story they tell is one of terrible stark medieval horror. It's like going back in time to something unimaginable from beginning to end of what they say, of being bodies in a container suffocating to death, waking up to find everyone around you dead, to being tortured in a prison in Afghanistan, being interrogated with a gun to your head, being transported like animals to a country you don't know where you are, and being treated like animals from start to finish for two years.

I think perhaps we're very calloused. We read, we watch, we hear about atrocities – we know what man's inhumanity to man consists of, we know all that, but we don't sufficiently register it. We don't have the capacity to take it in and react in the way we should as human beings. But when you have [in front of you] men you're getting to know and they're talking about it, not because you're interrogating them, but it's tumbling out and they're reminding each other, they're telling things that they haven't told anyone. Maybe it's the testimony of every survivor from a concentration camp or a massacre or a… How do you tell it? How do ordinary words tell it? But yet they do, if you are realising the people who are telling it to you are the people who've survived it, and there isn't any… I'm sorry, I'm not able to convey this to you well…

It is happening to our children, in that sense, yes, it's happening to our children and, perhaps, the disguising feature of it is the absolute lack of any artifice, or pretence, or contrivance, so that the words come tumbling out [from] young men who were busy at the same time looking at their new mobile phone, and seeing…trying to work out how it works. It's a complete ordinariness of where they are now, suddenly, from something so extraordinary. It's as if they've come from another planet.

Pause.

[There's] two contradictions. [There's] Guantanamo where there is continuous interrogation for the purposes of making people talk. [And there's] the converse here under internment [in Belmarsh] where 16 foreign nationals have been certificated by the Home Secretary since December 2001 as requiring to be detained indefinitely without trial [and] none of the[se] people have been asked a single question, they're simply locked up.

CLIVE STAFFORD SMITH: Belmarsh undercuts our ability to be patronising to the Americans when we're doing the same thing. It's shocking, the [idea] that somehow because you're a foreigner you are more dangerous than a British person. Let's assume we buy into the whole process that [they have done something wrong]: then you try them for it. If they didn't, then you don't. The concept that we can just detain people is just like *Minority Report*, I mean [it's as if] we're going to predict that these people are going to be violent in the future.

GARETH PEIRCE: What Blunkett wants for everybody accused of terrorism, he wants to abolish jury trials, have judge only, half of it in secret. He's on the way, yes. I think that Guantanamo is an experiment in how you obtain information from people and it's an experiment in whether anyone is going to protest about that.

JAMAL AL-HARITH: It made me stronger. Made me stronger but it opened my eyes, sometimes I do think it's a war on Muslims, a war on Islam. That came to mind when I was over there.

MR BEGG: If my son has done anything wrong he should be brought back to this country. Let him see his wife, his children and us. Let him be normal. If he is [medically and physically] alright take him to court, and let the court decide whether he is guilty or not. If he is guilty he should be punished. If he is not guilty he shouldn't be there for a second.

GREG POWELL: [There are] many features inside the criminal justice system which allows government to exercise very powerful social control from different areas of criminal law. Take football hooligans – football hooliganism established the right to take away your passport, the right to make you report to the Police Station on certain days, and the right to ban you from travelling abroad and attending some certain social functions; Anti-Social Behaviour Orders aimed at children on estates establish a whole series of things; Anti-Social Behaviour [Orders] can be for life, it can be that you are not allowed to speak to a named list of people or associate with them, you are not allowed to meet in public with more than two or three people at a time, and you must stay out of a quarantined area, a geographical area. Releasing prisoners on licence introduces home detention curfews and tagging, so you must stay at a certain place between certain hours. And finally [there's] prisoners staying in Guantanamo Bay and Belmarsh without trial.

It does not take a genius to add these together [and] you slightly reinvent the world. It means that if you fall under suspicion, you can be subject to a special tribunal, you can be, not necessarily, incarcerated for a long period of time, but you can be made subject to special measures if you like, and you could be electronically tagged, you could be denied access to certain people, you could be put in a certain geographical area, you could be limited where you go. All those features that I just described can be made applicable to you, so effectively you have this fantastic level of social control by some individuals inside the community. And having done it to terrorists…you can just extend it to the whole population of people who upset you because they commit crimes. So you can enter a whole new era of social control.

You can't start to think like this unless something like Guantanamo exists. In a way is an experiment but it leads you on into a much more controlling social control criminal justice system.

MR BEGG: I have quite a lot of letters [from Moazzam]. A lot have been lost. In the beginning I didn't bother about them because I think well he's coming out in a month or two or three or maybe four – so I didn't keep track. But I've got ten or eleven letters.
[In his letters] he didn't mention anything about er his life there, he talked his normal. [Then] one day I wrote [to him. I wrote, my heart is better now] I am absolutely alright, I go to the park, I walk, I do so many things which I could [not] do before and…er there is nothing wrong with me.

After this we received a letter that [is always] on my mind. Because he wrote in reply to my letter, Dad I'm pleased to know that you're well…and you can do so many things, but my situation is different. I've been treated like an animal. Most of the time I'm in chains and they throw me into cells or what do you call it…

MR BEGG, choking back tears.

I'm thinking something that is cell but is not cell –[yes, not cells,] cages –

As he tries to bite back his tears the caged MOAZZAM reads this letter.

MOAZZAM: Dear Dad,
As Salaam Aleikum
I received your message and am glad to hear all is well with you and the family. It is nearing a complete year since I have been in custody and I believe…that there has been a gross violation of my human rights, particularly to that right of freedom and innocence until

proven guilty. After all this time I still don't know what crime I am supposed to have committed for which not only I, but my wife and children should continually suffer for as a result. I am in a state of desperation and am beginning to lose the fight against depression and hopelessness. Whilst I do not at all complain about my personal treatments, conditions are such that I have not seen the sun, sky, moon etc for nearly a year!

MOAZZAM mouthing (censored words).

since it is the same three times a day, everyday – for all the time that I've been here! My situation here is unique in so many ways – for 'good' and 'bad' but mostly bad. I believe it is wrong for me to be kept like this and I have more than served enough time for whatever has been perceived about me, yet I still see no end in sight.

MOAZZAM mouthing (censored words)

and passed to

MOAZZAM mouthing (censored words).

I hate so much to place this burden upon you, and do as a last resort to alleviate this injustice. Please remember me in your prayers. Your son, Moazzam.

MR BEGG: (*Wiping tears away.*) [I have another letter.]

MOAZZAM: As-salaama 'alaykum.

MR BEGG: ...that means, 'Peace be upon you'.

MOAZZAM: I 'eid...wa barakaat Ramadan.

MR BEGG: ...that means congratulations for the festival... and Ramadan blessings.

MOAZZAM: Dear dad, I hope and pray all is well with you and the family. I am in receipt of your ICRC messages and I'm glad to hear that all is sound. I have written countless ICRC messages and letters by US mail to you (list of inaudible names). I expect that after this 'bombardment'…

MR BEGG: Letters he means…

MOAZZAM: Bombardment of news, I have 'inflicted' upon the authorities here, that some may found their way to you. My experience thus far however, has left me to believe that much of my mail to and from home has been deliberately constrained.

Including even, pictures of the family. I have yet to receive them father. I have not received any communication that was brought over by the visiting British delegation despite the fact that they informed me that they were hand over

MOAZZAM mouthing (censored words).

to all the family, Moazzam

please forward my greetings to T and others.

MR BEGG: This is the last letter I received.
He wrote it in 2003.
I received this one about two weeks [ago] I think.
[in March 2004]
Sometimes [the Foreign Office) tell us on telephone that [Moazzam's] alright, he sends you regards and all that but I don't know whether his hands are working, or his eyes are working or his brain is working because today I hear that they were giving injections to detainees.

[The Red Cross] say that the Censor Board is not letting us have the letters.

GARETH PEIRCE: We know that Moazzam Begg is in solitary confinement, we know he's been in solitary confinement since he was designated as an enemy combatant last summer. We have very good reason to think he's been driven into mental illness from oblique and unattributable comments that have been made to us – not by our Government, not by the American Government, but we believe that he is in a very bad way now and that's what this letter is saying. We believe he's in a very bad way.

CLIVE STAFFORD SMITH: He has confessed, apparently, Moazzam Begg, to being an Al-Qaeda agent who was going to take part in a plot to send an unmanned drone aircraft from somewhere in Suffolk to drop anthrax on the House of Commons. That's the confession right. Now what do you think? You as the jury. Do you feel that that's a credible allegation?

[I say] if you believe that, you believe in the tooth fairy… Number one, the only people who have drone aircraft in the world are the Americans, they cost $50 million each, they don't ever hit the target anyway and if you want to drop anthrax on someone, you just stick it in the damn air-conditioning system, and the whole thing is ludicrous… Now you think about what happened to the Tipton lads and you see the incredible good fortune that they had, because they confessed to being at the Al-Farouq training camp – every single person I've come across so far has confessed to being in the Al-Farouq training camp, they must have had millions of people in it at one point – and they confessed to being there in 2000. And the Americans got very excited when they confessed to that, they put them in a solitary cell and were getting all fixed to prosecute them for being vicious Al-Qaeda terrorists. Well fortunately, and purely by good fortune, MI5 checked the story for the US. [And they] proved that they really weren't in the Al-Farouq training camp, they were working in Currys in Birmingham at the time. So the reason those kids didn't get charged with that and they got let out of the whole solitary confinement, was that purely by fortune an alibi was proven.

MAJOR MORI: [I am a Defence Counsel at the Military Commissions. My client, an Australian, who will be one of the first of four cases against Guantanamo detainees for violating the law of war.] I was working as a Head Prosecutor for the Marines [when I got this job]. It was half a challenge, half just wanting to find out if it really was going to be like they were planning.

The US Court Martial system is an efficient and fair criminal justice system [that has] jurisdiction to try Law of War violations and its rules and procedures specifically gear to battlefield type cases. [But] all of a sudden you see this step back to before the Geneva Convention has come into play. [These Guantanamo military commissions are] doing away with all the safe guards and checks and balances in the justice system that are there to ensure that innocent people aren't convicted. I don't understand it. It seems very contrary to fundamental fairnesses. In my introduction to the Military, and through my legal training, these are very basic protections that are needed in the justice system. You need to have an independent judge, you need an independent review process. The system can't be controlled by people with a vested interest only in convictions.

One of my fears is that they're not going to bring someone just to testify against my client, they are going to bring some document written by some investigator of what Mr Smith told him, and they are going to use this document, and I'm never going to have the opportunity to cross [examine] Mr Smith, all the fundamental protections of a fair trial have been removed.

The problem with this system [is] it's not a justice system, it's a political system.

MR BEGG: [This] is a human rights issue. I'm not asking mercy from anybody. I am asking justice.

MAJOR MORI: I worry about [not being able to do my duty to my client properly]. There is no independent judge in this process, and our criminal justice system both in the Military and the Civilian in America has recognised that you need an independent judge to serve certain functions to ensure that there's a fair system, that both sides get an equal shot at putting on their case, and equal access to evidence, that there is an independent person not part of the prosecution to rule on motions.

MR BEGG: Justice in process. Justice. Human rights justice.

GARETH PEIRCE: I would like to be wrong, but with the people we represent [in Belmarsh] we don't want to mislead them. [They] want to know, can I win my appeal? [They] want to know, is there any point me participating in the process? They want to know, our case is going to the House of Lords, is there any hope? Will I see my wife and children again in the foreseeable future, or is this it? And one has to be truthful at the same time as wanting to give hope, it isn't right to give false hope, and it's that growing feeling, knowledge, not just feeling, knowledge that you're not meant to get out of this and that you might be there forever and the feeling that if you were not a good Muslim who found the concept of killing yourself abhorrent, that you might be going on the view that your wife and children, for instance, might be better off without you…

MAJOR MORI: When they let the [five] Britons go home, and the Foreign Secretary, Mr Straw said that the remaining four should either receive a trial under international legal standards, or should be returned home. That was a very strong stand… Well, I'm telling you I really think it's up to Britain. It's up to Britain if they're going to tolerate this sub-standard form of justice for people…

LORD JUSTICE STEYN: At Guantanamo Bay arrangements for the trials are proceeding with great efficiency. A court room with an execution chamber nearby has apparently been constructed. But the British prisoners will not be liable to be executed. The Attorney-General has negotiated a separate agreement with the Pentagon on the treatment of British prisoners. He has apparently received a promise that the British prisoners of war will not face the death penalty. This gives a new dimension to the concept of 'most favoured nation' treatment in international law. How could it be morally defensible to discriminate in this way between individual prisoners? It lifts the curtain a little on the arbitrariness of what is happening at Guantanamo Bay, and in the corridors of power on both sides of the Atlantic […]

The question is whether the quality of justice envisaged for the prisoners at Guantanamo Bay complies with minimum international standards for the conduct of fair trials. The answer can be given quite shortly: It is a resounding No […]

Trials of the type contemplated by the United States government would be a stain on United States justice. The only thing that could be worse is simply to leave the prisoners in their black hole indefinitely […]

The type of justice meted out at Guantanamo Bay is likely to make martyrs of the prisoners in the moderate Muslim world with whom the West must work to ensure world peace and stability […]

It may be appropriate to pose a question: ought our government to make plain publicly and unambiguously our condemnation of the utter lawlessness at Guantanamo Bay?

John Donne, who preached in the Chapel of Lincoln's Inn, gave the context of the question more than four centuries ago:

'No man is an Island, entire of it self; every man is a piece of the Continent, a part of the main;…any man's death diminishes me, because I am involved in Mankind; And therefore never send to know for whom the bell tolls; it tolls for thee.'

Call to prayer: Isha: sung from the stage.

Text on dot matrix – or a voice over:

VOICE: UK citizens Feroz Abassi, Moazzam Begg, Richard Belmar and Martin Mubanga, and UK residents Bisher al-Rawi and Jamil Al-Banna are among more than 650 prisoners held in Guantanamo. Most are from countries with even less power than Britain to influence events. They are being held indefinitely.

End.